FOOTBALL STARS

MIKE RYAN

FIREFLY BOOKS

A FIREFLY BOOK

Published by Firefly Books Ltd. 2018

First printing

Library of Congress Control Number: 2018941776

Library and Archives Canada Cataloguing in Publication
Ryan, Mike, 1974-, author
    Football stars / Mike Ryan.

ISBN 978-0-228-10073-7 (hardcover).--ISBN 978-0-228-10072-0 (softcover)

    1. Football players--Biography--Juvenile literature. 2. Football--
Juvenile literature. 3. National Football League--Juvenile literature.
I. Title.

GV939.A1R935 2018   j796.332092'2   C2018-902299-X

Published in the United States by
Firefly Books (U.S.) Inc.
P.O. Box 1338, Ellicott Station
Buffalo, New York 14205

Published in Canada by
Firefly Books Ltd.
50 Staples Avenue, Unit 1
Richmond Hill, Ontario L4B 0A7

Cover and interior design: Kimberley Young

Printed in China

Canada We acknowledge the financial support of the Government of Canada.

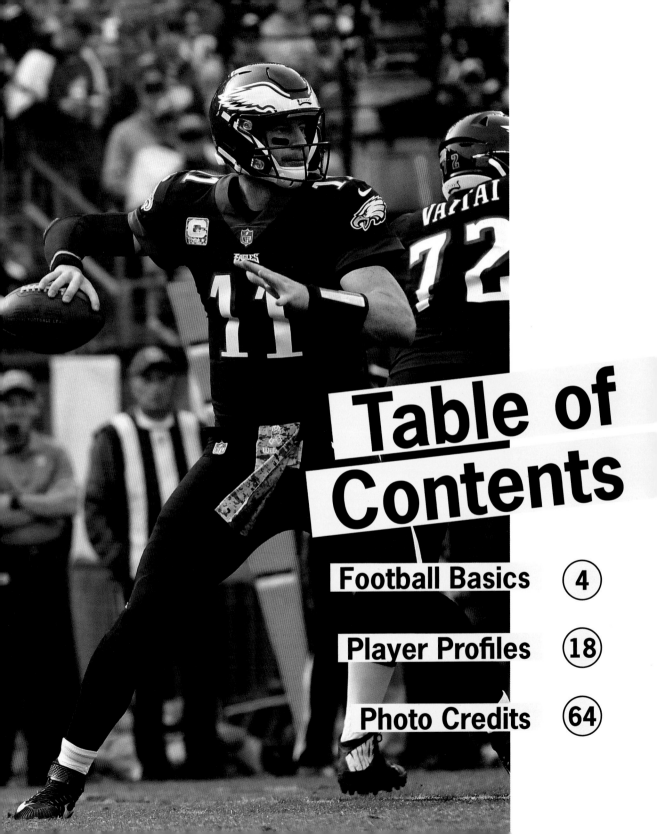

Table of Contents

Football
Basics

Nuts and Bolts

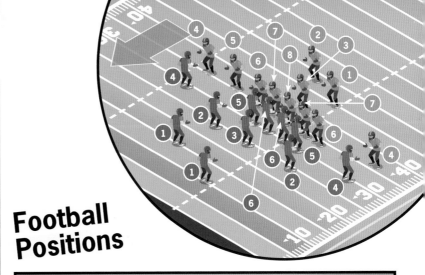

BY THE NUMBERS

11 The maximum number of players each team can have on the field at any one time

53 The maximum number of players on an NFL roster

46 The maximum number of players on a game-day roster

TIME

GAME TIME – 60 minutes split into four 15-minute quarters (In the regular season 10-minute overtime quarters are added as needed)

SEASON – 16 games in an NFL season

PLAYOFFS – 4 is the most playoff games a team needs to play to win the Super Bowl; 3 games is the fewest

Football Positions

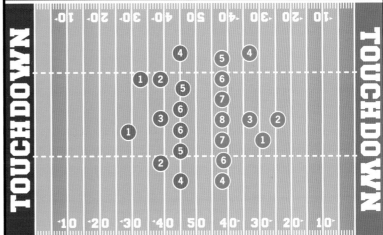

DEFENSE

1 **Safety** – Covers passes and stops runs

2 **Outside Linebacker** – Covers passes and blitzes

3 **Middle Linebacker** – Manages the defense, covers passes, stops runs and rushes the quarterback

4 **Cornerback** – Covers passes

5 **Defensive End** – Rushes the quarterback and stops runs on the edge

6 **Defensive Tackle** – Rushes the quarterback and stops runs up the middle

OFFENSE

1 **Fullback** – Blocks for the running back, receives and runs with the ball

2 **Running Back** – Runs with the ball

3 **Quarterback** – Throws the ball, hands the ball off and runs with the ball

4 **Wide Receiver** – Catches the ball

5 **Tight End** – Catches and runs with the ball

6 **Tackle** – Blocks

7 **Guard** – Blocks

8 **Center** – Snaps the ball and blocks

POINTS

6 **TOUCHDOWN**
Accomplished by running the ball into the end zone or catching the ball in the end zone.

3 **FIELD GOAL**
Accomplished by kicking the ball, which is held in place against the ground by another player, through the goalposts.

2 **TWO-POINT CONVERSION**
(following a touchdown)
Accomplished by running the ball into the end zone or catching the ball in the end zone.

1 **POINT AFTER ATTEMPT**
(following a touchdown)
Accomplished by kicking the ball, which is held in place against the ground by another player, through the goalposts.

2 **SAFETY**
Accomplished by tackling the ball carrier in his own end zone, as a consequence of the offense committing a foul in their own end zone or the ball becoming dead in the offense's end zone (with the exception of an incomplete forward pass).

Football has a language of its own! Here are some terms you might hear the next time you watch a game.

BLITZ: When the defense sends extra players to overwhelm the offensive line and sack the quarterback.

COFFIN CORNER: Named after an area built into old Victorian homes; it's where the sideline meets the goal line. Punters attempt to pin the receiving team there.

FLEA FLICKER: When the quarterback hands the ball off to a running back, who then throws it back to the quarterback.

HAIL MARY: A desperate, last-ditch attempt to throw a touchdown. Typically, all players run to the end zone, and the ball is up for grabs.

ICING THE KICKER: When the defensive team calls a time-out immediately before a kicker attempts a field goal. It's a psychological tactic used to make the kicker nervous.

SHOTGUN: An offensive formation in which the quarterback takes a few steps back from the line of scrimmage to receive the snap. This formation spreads receivers all over the field.

WILDCAT: An offensive formation in which the quarterback lines up as a wide receiver and a running back or wide receiver receives the snap.

LEARN THE LINGO

TOUCHDOWN

-10 -20 -30 -0
-10 -20 -30 -40

120 yd (109.7 m/360 ft) – length of the field, including end zones

The Field

First Down – teams are given four downs (attempts) to move the ball 10 yards (or more) in the direction of their opponent's end zone. Every time they move the ball 10 yards, they are rewarded with another four downs to move the ball 10 more yards. If a team fails to move 10 yards in four downs, it is called a "turnover on downs," and the other team gets the ball. The yards needed to achieve a first down are marked by the orange and black yard markers.

THE BALL

Wilson has been the official supplier of balls since 1941, and since 1955, all NFL balls have been made at the Wilson factory in Ada, Ohio. They're made from cowhide from Kansas, Nebraska and Iowa; each cowhide can make about 10 balls. Each ball has four panels and a synthetic bladder to hold air. There is one lace for grip, going through 16 lace holes. Each ball is between 11 and 11¼ inches (28–28.5 cm) long and weighs between 14 and 15 ounces (400–425 grams). It should be inflated to 13 psi. Each team is given 108 game balls per week: 54 for practice and 54 for the game.

18.6 ft (5.7 m) – distance between goalposts

20 ft (6 m) – height of goalposts

10 ft (3 m) – distance of goalposts from the ground

OFFICIALS

There are seven officials who call each NFL game:

- referee
- umpire
- head linesman
- line judge
- field judge
- side judge
- back judge

TOUCHDOWN

53.3 yd (48.8 m/160 ft) – width of the field

100 yd (91.4 m/300 ft) – length of the field, goal line to goal line

NFL Fun!

HEIGHT

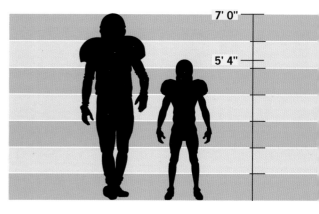

7' 0"

5' 4"

Tallest
Richard Sligh
(Oakland Raiders, 1967):
7-foot-0 (2.1 m)

Shortest (after 1930)
Reggie Smith
(Atlanta Falcons,
New York Jets, 1980–87):
5-foot-4 (1.6 m)

WEIGHT

Heaviest
Aaron Gibson (Detroit Lions,
Dallas Cowboys, Chicago
Bears, 1999–2004):
410 pounds (186 kg)

Lightest (after 1930)
Tad Weed (Pittsburgh
Steelers, 1955): 140 pounds
(64 kg)

Super Bowl Stats

$50,000, 22 and 7 – the cost, height (in inches) and weight (in pounds) of the Vince Lombardi Trophy, made by Tiffany and Co. and given to the Super Bowl champions

Teams with the Most Super Bowl Victories

Pittsburgh Steelers: 🏆 🏆 🏆 🏆 🏆 🏆

Dallas Cowboys: 🏆 🏆 🏆 🏆 🏆

New England Patriots: 🏆 🏆 🏆 🏆 🏆

San Francisco 49ers: 🏆 🏆 🏆 🏆 🏆

Quiz Time!

1. What is the NFL's oldest team?

   a) Green Bay Packers

   b) Arizona Cardinals

   c) Chicago Bears

   d) Pittsburgh Steelers

2. What does the "G" on the Packers' helmets stand for?

   a) Green Bay

   b) Gridiron

   c) Goal

   d) Greatness

3. How many NFL teams play in New York state?

   a) 1

   b) 2

   c) 3

   d) 4

4. Who is the NFL's all-time leading scorer?

   a) Jerry Rice

   b) Morten Andersen

   c) Peyton Manning

   d) Gary Anderson

5. What is the longest regular-season winning streak in NFL history?

   a) 16 games

   b) 19 games

   c) 23 games

   d) 31 games

6. Which NFL stadium has the most seats?

   a) Soldier Field

   b) Los Angeles Memorial Coliseum

   c) MetLife Stadium

   d) Mercedes-Benz Superdome

Quiz Time! Answers

1. **b)** In 1899 the Morgan Athletic Club on the south side of Chicago formed a team. It later became the Normals, the Racine Cardinals, the Chicago Cardinals, the St. Louis Cardinals, the Phoenix Cardinals and the Arizona Cardinals — the oldest continuously running team in pro football.

2. **d)** In 1961 equipment manager George Braishear came up with the familiar logo, but the letter represented "greatness." It worked: Green Bay won the first two Super Bowls. The University of Georgia liked it so much that they used the same logo for their helmets.

3. **a)** Only the Buffalo Bills play in the state of New York. Both the Giants and the Jets play at the MetLife Stadium in East Rutherford, New Jersey.

4. **b)** Morten Andersen, known as "The Great Dane," passed Gary Anderson (both were kickers), to become the NFL's all-time leader in points scored with 2,544. Kickers rack up points with field goals and touchdown conversions (point after). Since they play a less physical role, they also have longer careers. Hall of Famer Andersen also holds the NFL record for games played at 382 over 25 seasons. Indianapolis Colts kicker Adam Vinatieri is currently second in points scored; he's been playing for 22 seasons.

5. **c)** Peyton Manning and the Indianapolis Colts won 23 straight regular-season games over the 2008 and 2009 seasons. In the modern NFL, the only teams to go undefeated in one regular season are the 1972 Miami Dolphins (14-0) and the 2007 New England Patriots (16-0). New England also has a 31-game home winning streak.

6. **b)** The temporary home of the Los Angeles Rams, the Los Angeles Memorial Coliseum has 93,607 seats for football games. It hosted Super Bowls I and VII and the 1932 and 1984 Olympics. The Rams played there from 1946 to 1979, before they relocated to Anaheim Stadium and then to St. Louis in 1995. They returned to Los Angeles and the Coliseum in 2016. In 2019 the name will officially change to the United Airlines Memorial Coliseum, and it's slated to host the Olympics again in 2028.

Half a Foot Equals 63 Yards?

On November 8, 1970, Tom Dempsey of the New Orleans Saints won the game for his team and set the NFL record with a 63-yard field goal. Setting the record was one thing, but Dempsey did it with a kicking foot that was misshapen at birth and was more of a stump than a foot! The record wasn't broken until 2013, when Matt Prater of the Denver Broncos beat it by one yard.

Did You Know...

A "Gridiron" Is a Field?

In the early days of the game, the lines on the field were more of a grid, like a checkerboard. They looked like the lines on a griddle (the kind used to make waffles), which is the original meaning of the word gridiron. In other countries people sometimes call American football "gridiron football" to avoid confusion with football, which North Americans call soccer.

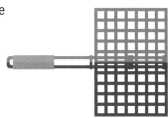

The Inventor of the Huddle Was Deaf?

Paul Hubbard was the quarterback for Gallaudet University (a school for the deaf and hard of hearing in Washington, D.C.). In the 1940s he invented the huddle to make sure that other teams couldn't read their sign language. The huddle is still being used in the NFL.

Football Through Time!

1919
Earl "Curly" Lambeau and George Calhoun form the Green Bay Packers. Lambeau's employer, the Indian Packing Company, provides equipment and a practice field.

1876
The first rules are created for football.

1920
The American Professional Football Association is formed after two meetings are held in Canton, Ohio.

1906
Players are allowed to pass the ball forward.

1921
Earl Akron Pros player–coach Fritz Pollard becomes the first African-American head coach.

1869
Princeton University and Rutgers University face off in a game of "soccer football" using modified rugby rules.

1892
William "Pudge" Heffelfinger becomes the first player paid to play football: $500 by the Allegheny Athletic Association.

1929

Ernie Nevers scores six rushing touchdowns and four extra points for a total of 40 points. It is still the NFL record for most points by one player in a single game.

1933

The NFL adds inbound lines, hash marks and goalposts on the goal line. They also legalize the forward pass from anywhere behind the line of scrimmage.

1936

The NFL holds its first draft of college players. Heisman Trophy—winner Jay Berwanger is the first player ever drafted. He never plays in the NFL.

1925

Five new franchises join the NFL, including the New York Giants, owned by Tim Mara. The Mara family still owns the Giants.

1922

The American Professional Football Association becomes the National Football League, and the Chicago Staleys change their name to the Chicago Bears.

1932

Chicago and Portsmouth play in the first NFL playoff game; because of terrible snow and cold, they play indoors at Chicago Stadium.

1934

The Chicago—Detroit Thanksgiving Day game is the first NFL game to be broadcast nationally on the radio.

1939

The first televised NFL game is broadcast by NBC. About 1,000 TV sets in New York show the Brooklyn Dodgers playing the Philadelphia Eagles.

1943

The NFL makes helmets mandatory.

1963

The Pro Football Hall of Fame opens in Canton, Ohio, with 17 members enshrined.

1965

Americans choose professional football as their favorite sport, overtaking baseball for the first time.

1948

The NFL gives its referees whistles instead of horns.

1939

The first Pro Bowl, between the NFL-champion New York Giants and a team of All-Stars, is played. The Giants win 13–10.

1956

The NFL Players' Association is formed.

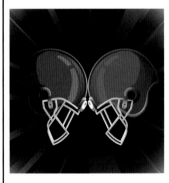

1959

The rival American Football League is founded with eight franchises.

1948

Fred Gehrke of the Los Angeles Rams paints horns on the Rams' helmets; the Rams become the first professional team to have helmet emblems.

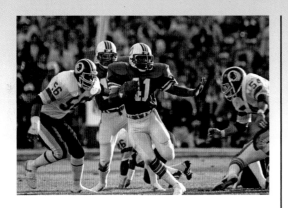

1983

Super Bowl XVII is the second-highest rated live TV program of all time, giving the NFL all of the top-10 live programs in TV history.

1978

The regular season becomes 16 games long, and the NFL adds a second wild-card team to the playoffs.

1970

Monday Night Football debuts.

1988

Johnny Grier becomes the first African-American referee in NFL history.

1970

Vince Lombardi dies, and the Super Bowl Trophy is renamed the Vince Lombardi Trophy.

1989

Art Shell is named head coach of the Los Angeles Raiders, becoming the first African-American head coach since Fritz Pollard in 1921.

1967

The NFL and AFL merge, and the NFL's Green Bay Packers beat the AFL's Kansas City Chiefs in Super Bowl I.

1986

The telecast of Super Bowl XX becomes the most-viewed television program in history, with an audience of 127 million viewers.

1993

The Miami Dolphins' Don Shula becomes the winningest coach in NFL history.

2014

Manning becomes the NFL's all-time leader in career touchdown passes.

2009

The Pittsburgh Steelers win their record sixth Super Bowl title.

1995

The San Francisco 49ers become the first team to win five Super Bowls, and the NFL becomes the first major sports league to have a website on the Internet.

2002

The Dallas Cowboys' Emmitt Smith becomes the NFL's all-time rushing leader.

2013

The Denver Broncos' Peyton Manning breaks the single-season records for passing yards (5,477) and touchdowns (55). He also becomes the first five-time NFL MVP.

2017

At Super Bowl LI, Tom Brady and the New England Patriots come back from a 28–3 deficit in the third quarter to win 34–28. It's the biggest comeback in Super Bowl history and the first Super Bowl overtime. Brady wins his record fourth Super Bowl MVP award.

2015

Manning breaks the NFL record for career passing yards.

2016

On February 7, Super Bowl 50 is played. It's the first time roman numerals aren't used for the Super Bowl. Peyton Manning's Broncos beat MVP Cam Newton and the Carolina Panthers 24–10.

2018

The Patriots and the Philadelphia Eagles set a record for total yards in any NFL game — regular season or playoff — with 1,151. In a game with only one punt, Brady sets a playoff record with 505 yards passing, but the Eagles win 41–33.

Player Profiles

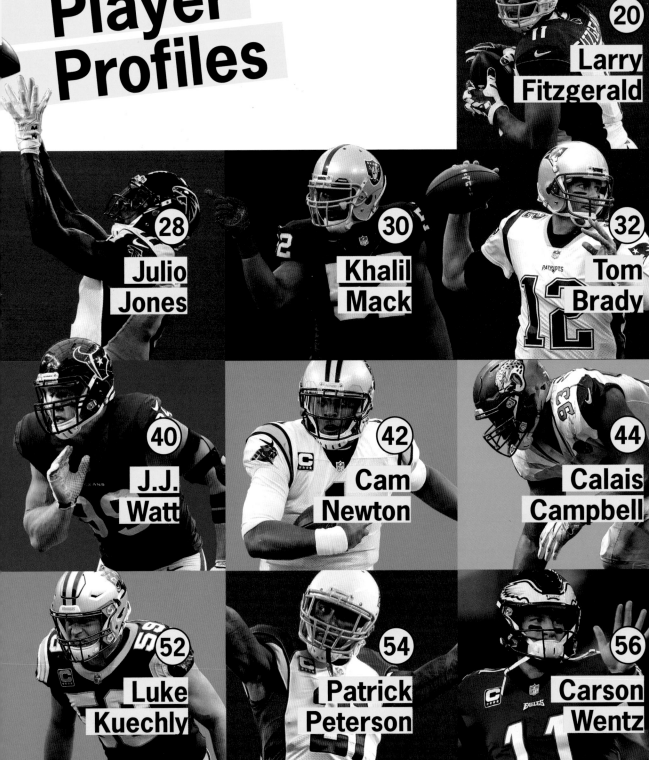

20 Larry Fitzgerald

28 Julio Jones

30 Khalil Mack

32 Tom Brady

40 J.J. Watt

42 Cam Newton

44 Calais Campbell

52 Luke Kuechly

54 Patrick Peterson

56 Carson Wentz

22 Von Miller

24 Drew Brees

26 Richard Sherman

34 Todd Gurley II

36 Cameron Jordan

38 Matthew Stafford

46 Aaron Rodgers

48 Odell Beckham Jr.

50 Russell Wilson

58 Tyron Smith

60 Matt Ryan

62 Antonio Brown

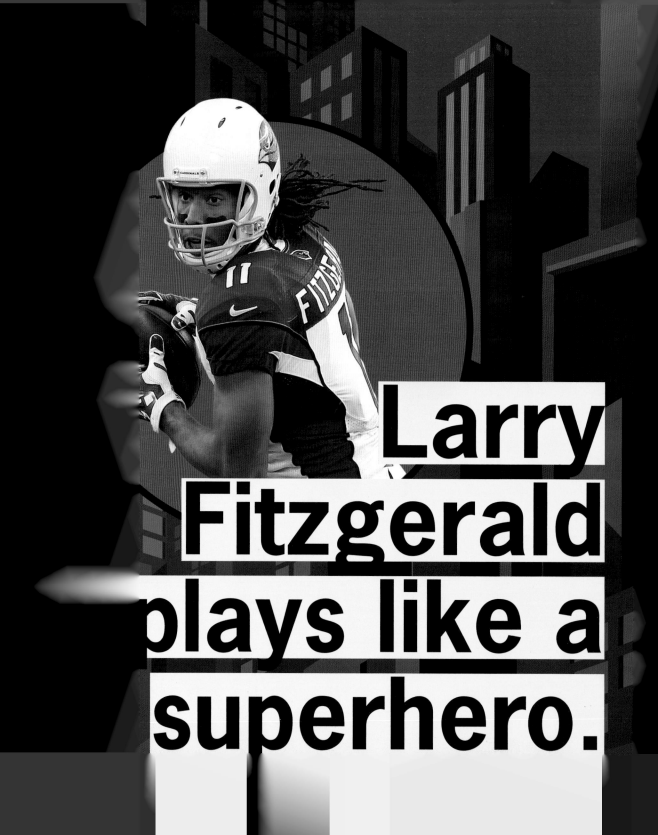

Larry Fitzgerald plays like a superhero.

Larry Fitzgerald
Arizona Cardinals
Wide Receiver

Larry Fitzgerald plays like a superhero on the football field. The wide receiver is known as "Spidey" for his sticky palms, which help him make spectacular catches, but he could also be called "Wolverine" for his ability to play through pain and heal quickly after injuries.

Fitzgerald's extraordinary powers were first revealed to the football world when he was in college. Playing for the Pittsburgh Panthers in 2003, he was named the best wide receiver in NCAA football — and he did it with a torn ligament in his right hand.

The Arizona Cardinals liked the tough, sure-handed wideout, and they drafted him third overall in 2004. By the end of the 2005 season, Spidey was the youngest receiver in NFL history to reach 100 receptions. His total of 103 set a Cardinals team record.

In 2008 Fitzgerald became just the fourth receiver in NFL history to have at least 1,400 receiving yards in three or more seasons. In that year's playoffs he took his game to the next level, setting all-time NFL playoff records for catches (30), yards (546), touchdowns (seven) and touchdown catches in consecutive games (four).

But in the last 11 minutes of Super Bowl XLIII, he was truly superb. Fitzgerald caught six passes for 115 yards and two touchdowns. Only one receiver had more yards in an entire game against the Pittsburgh Steelers that whole season! Fitzgerald's second touchdown gave the Cardinals a 23–20 lead with 2:37 left in the game, but Arizona ultimately lost.

Fitzgerald revealed that, unbelievably, he set

his records with a broken left thumb and torn cartilage in his left hand.

Fitzgerald shares more than his sticky palms and nickname with the blue and red webslinger: like Spider-Man, he lost a loved one when he was younger. His mom died when he was in college, and he hasn't cut his hair since. He braids it as a tribute to her.

His other superpower appears to be immunity to aging. Fitzgerald led the NFL with 107 receptions in 2016 and tied a career high with 109 in 2017. It was his third straight year with over 1,000 yards receiving, and the ninth time he achieved that feat in his career. He was also named to his 11th Pro Bowl!

The co-winner of the 2016 Walter Payton Man of the Year Award now sits first among active players — and third in NFL history — in receptions (1,234) and receiving yards (15,545), as well as second in touchdowns (110) and yards from scrimmage (15,613).

But as the legend and future Hall of Famer says, "It's not all about football. You have to be a good citizen and give back to people less fortunate. Those are things my parents taught me."

SUPER DUDE

In an NFL player vote, Fitzgerald was named as one of the nicest guys in the league. His First Down Fund fixes fields and donates sports equipment in Minnesota and gives laptops to kids in Minneapolis and Phoenix. He also runs the Carol Fitzgerald Memorial Fund, in honor of his mother, to support breast cancer awareness.

Von Miller
Denver Broncos
Outside Linebacker

Vonnie B'Vsean Miller was built to play football. At 6-foot-3 and 250 pounds, he has a rare blend of speed and power that allows him to get to opposing quarterbacks with finesse or force.

Better known as Von, Miller grew up in DeSoto, Texas. He was a football prodigy who got by on raw talent at Texas A&M University, until former Green Bay Packers coach Mike Sherman came along.

One of Sherman's first acts was to suspend Miller indefinitely, or until he started taking practices and his schoolwork seriously. Miller considered transferring, but his father reminded him he'd made a commitment to the school and the team.

Miller put in the work and was welcomed back as a hybrid defensive end/outside linebacker, a position called "joker." He led the country with 17 sacks in his junior year, and as a senior he won the Butkus Award as the country's best linebacker.

After being drafted second overall in 2011 by the Denver Broncos, Miller was named to the All-Pro and Pro Bowl teams and won Defensive Rookie of the Year.

In 2012 Miller set a Broncos single-season record with 18.5 sacks, and he was runner-up for Defensive Player of the Year.

Prior to the 2013 season, Miller was ranked the ninth-best player in the league by the NFL Network. However, he tore his ACL in the second-last game of the regular season, and he had to watch as the Broncos reached Super Bowl XLVIII. Without him in the lineup, the Seattle Seahawks ran over the Denver defense in a 43–8 victory.

Miller attacked his rehab and lost weight so he could be more explosive and put less stress on his joints. He played all 16 games in 2014 and had 14.0 sacks and 59 tackles. His dominance continued in 2015 as the Broncos reached Super Bowl 50. Miller had six tackles, two quarterback hits, a pass defended and two forced fumbles against the Carolina Panthers. He also had 2.5 sacks of quarterback Cam Newton, the only player picked ahead of him in the 2011 draft.

The Broncos won 24–10, and Miller was named Super Bowl MVP. He was just the third linebacker and the 10th defensive player in history to win the award.

Before the 2017 season, Miller moved up the NFL Network's list of the best players, ranking second. He lived up to the honor, with his sixth Pro Bowl and sixth All-Pro team nods.

"He's a hell of a player," says Gary Kubiak, Broncos senior personnel advisor and former coach, "but he has become a great pro, a great man and a big leader on this football team."

SMELL GOOD, LOOK GOOD, PLAY GOOD

Miller is the face of an Old Spice campaign, and *Sports Illustrated* named him one of the 50 most fashionable people in sports (and the "most accessorized").

Von Miller is absolutely smashing.

Drew Brees
New Orleans Saints
Quarterback

At the end of the 2005 NFL season, a lot of people thought Drew Brees' career was over. Playing for the San Diego Chargers, Brees had torn up his throwing shoulder in the last game of the season. Surgery fixed his arm, but the Chargers had quarterback-of-the-future Philip Rivers on the roster, so they released Brees from the team.

Earlier that year, Hurricane Katrina had devastated the city of New Orleans, killing almost 2,000 people. The New Orleans Saints' stadium had become a shelter for people who'd lost their homes, so the Saints were playing their home games away from home. They ended the 2005 season with a 3-13 record, but they signed Brees that offseason.

"[My wife and I] were brought here for a reason," Brees says. He and his wife, Brittany, rebuilt an old home in downtown New Orleans and started to help others rebuild their lives. They set up the Brees Dream Foundation, built playgrounds and repaired football fields.

And Brees' repaired shoulder turned the Saints around on the field — the team finished with a 10-6 record in 2006, and by the conclusion of the 2009 season, the Saints were Super Bowl champions. Super Bowl XLIV was New Orleans' first championship ever, and Brees won the MVP award!

The next season, Brees beat Dan Marino's 27-year-old single-season record for passing yards — with a game to spare. He finished the season with 5,476 yards and also set records for completions in a season (468) and completion percentage (71.2%).

Since arriving in New Orleans in 2006, Brees has only missed two games and leads the NFL in passing yards, completions and touchdowns. He's the most accurate passer in NFL history, and his streak of 54 consecutive games with a touchdown pass between 2009 and 2012 smashed a mark that had stood since 1960.

Brees also broke a record with nine consecutive seasons of at least 4,000 yards passing, which is now 12 seasons and counting. He is also the first quarterback in NFL history to throw 30 touchdowns in seven consecutive seasons, which he has since extended to nine seasons.

In 2017, at the age of 38, Brees led the NFL in completions (386) for the sixth time and completion percentage (72.0) for the fourth time. In addition to this collection of honors, which also includes two Offensive Player of the Year awards, a *Sports Illustrated* Sportsman of the Year award and an *AP* Male Athlete of the Year, he was named to his 11th Pro Bowl.

Most important to Brees, however, might be the NFL's Walter Payton Man of the Year Award he won in 2006. For the future Hall of Famer, helping rebuild New Orleans' shattered core and confidence is his greatest accomplishment.

SAY WHAT?

Brees is the only player in NFL history to throw for at least 5,000 yards in a season more than once. He's done it four times!

Drew Brees always hits his target.

Richard Sherman will take you to school.

Richard Sherman
San Francisco 49ers
Cornerback

"U mad bro?"

That was the tweet in 2012 that earned Richard Sherman thousands of followers and nearly as many enemies. It came after a game that saw the underdog Seattle Seahawks defeat the New England Patriots. At the time, Sherman's Seahawks were coming off a 7-9 season, and Sherman was a second-year unknown. The Patriots, on the other hand, were defending AFC champions and led by superstar quarterback Tom Brady.

After Seattle beat the Patriots, a picture of Sherman jawing with Brady was put on Twitter with the infamous caption added to it; Sherman later re-tweeted it.

Growing up in Compton, California, where the tradition and history of rap music helped shape his verbal game, Sherman steered clear of the Los Angeles neighborhood's notorious gang life by focusing on school and sports. His grades and athletic skill allowed him to attend Stanford University, a school known for demanding good grades. His idol was Muhammad Ali, and, like him, he wanted to have the same combination of athletic talent, sharp mind and social conscience.

Sherman graduated from Stanford with a degree in communications and was drafted in the fifth round by Seattle in 2011.

It hasn't all been smooth sailing, however. In the 2013 NFC title game against the San Francisco 49ers, Sherman broke up a pass intended for Michael Crabtree that sealed the game. After the play Sherman extended a hand to Crabtree, who pushed him away. Moments later, Sherman erupted on live TV: "Don't you ever talk about me. ... Don't you open your mouth about the best, or I'll shut it for you real quick."

In the aftermath, Sherman was labeled a "thug." He didn't apologize to Crabtree, but he was sorry for overshadowing his team and for putting the reporter in an awkward position. The Seahawks went on to beat the Denver Broncos in Super Bowl XLVIII.

Since entering the league in 2011, Sherman has amassed more interceptions (32) and passes defended (104) than any other player. He's been named a First Team All-Pro three times, and he's been to four Pro Bowls. He also played in 105 straight games before tearing his Achilles tendon in November 2017.

It was the end of his reign in the Emerald City. Seattle released Sherman, and he signed with the San Francisco 49ers. Proving he's as savvy off the field as on, he acted as his own agent.

"One of the main reasons I had decided to represent myself in negotiations was because I knew it would be a big challenge," said Sherman. "And I never shy away from a challenge."

25

TEAM SHERMAN | Sherman has students sign a contract with his foundation, Blanket Coverage. If they agree to improve their grades, keep up their attendance and are good citizens, he'll help them with clothes and school supplies.

Julio Jones soars over defenders.

Julio Jones
Atlanta Falcons
Wide Receiver

Quintorris Lopez Jones, better known as Julio, started pestering his mom to let him play football when he was five. Even though Quintorris means "gladiator," she was worried because he was smaller than the other kids playing in Foley, Alabama.

She didn't let him on the field until he was 12. By then the kid with the long legs and arms could dunk a basketball and excelled in whatever sport he tried.

At Foley High School, Jones had 194 catches for 3,287 yards and 43 touchdowns, shattering school records. As a senior he was named Alabama's "Mr. Football" and Gatorade Player of the Year.

Jones stayed close to home, going to the University of Alabama, and during three years with the Crimson Tide he caught 179 passes for 2,653 yards, both good for second in the school's history. He also won the national title as a sophomore and Alabama's Commitment to Academic Excellence Award twice.

"Everything that kid did was folklore," says Lance Thompson, an assistant coach who helped recruit Jones. "But everything you hear about him is accurate."

The Atlanta Falcons had their sights set on Jones and sent five picks to the Cleveland Browns to move up and draft him sixth overall in 2011. In 2013 he was leading the league in both receptions and yards when he broke his foot during the fifth game of the season. Healthy again in 2014, he set a single-game team record with 259 receiving yards against the Green Bay Packers — the most yards that storied franchise

has ever given up. His 1,593 yards that year set another Falcons record.

He broke that with 1,871 yards in 2015, which led the NFL, and he tied for first with 136 receptions. He's also one of only two players in NFL history with at least 136 catches and over 1,800 yards in a single season.

In 2016 Jones led the league with 100.6 yards per game. He also gained an incredible 300 yards against the Carolina Panthers. He was just the fourth player in the Super Bowl era (since 1967) with 300 yards in a game and the only one with two games of at least 250 yards.

After the regular season Jones had a spectacular tiptoe catch on the sideline in the fourth quarter of Super Bowl LI, but in the end the Falcons suffered a heartbreaking loss to the New England Patriots.

Jones added yet another game with 250-plus yards in 2017 (253 against the Tampa Bay Buccaneers). He also finished second in the league with 1,444 receiving yards and was chosen for his fifth Pro Bowl.

According to fellow Falcons receiver Taylor Gabriel, the secret to Jones' success is simple: "Julio is Julio. Superman."

GOING THE EXTRA YARDS

After seven seasons, Jones has averaged 95.3 receiving yards per game. No other player with at least four years in the NFL has cracked 87.0. He's also ranked first in playoff history with 104.3 yards per game.

Khalil Mack
Oakland Raiders
Defensive End

52

A t Westwood High School in Fort Pierce, Florida, Khalil Mack ran into some injury problems. The most serious was a torn patellar tendon in his left knee, limiting him to just one full season of football. He led his team in tackles that year, but he was only offered one scholarship, to the University of Buffalo. Mack traded southern sunshine for heavy snow.

Feeling ignored and underrated, Mack had a chip on his shoulder and a weighted vest on his chest while running sprints up the "Hill" beside the Bulls' stadium.

"Every time we ran up that hill, we got to the top, Khalil would remind us of what we were trying to get to, what we were trying to be," said college teammate Najja Johnson.

Mack arrived in Buffalo weighing 210 pounds, with just a 46 (out of 99) player rating in EA Sports' *NCAA Football 11* video game. He made 46 his jersey number and kept it throughout his college career as motivation.

Perks were limited at the smaller school, and Mack lived on Taco Bell for a while, thanks to a teammate who was a night manager at the fast food chain. But he was focused and a gym rat, and after five years he left Buffalo with an extra 35 pounds of muscle and the NCAA's all-time record of 16 forced fumbles. His 75 tackles for a loss also tied a modern-day NCAA record.

In a game against powerhouse Ohio State in his senior year, Mack returned an interception for a touchdown and had 2.5 sacks. Scouts took notice, and the Oakland Raiders made him the fifth overall pick in the 2014 NFL draft.

Mack made the 2014 All-Rookie Team as an outside linebacker, and in 2015 he was moved to defensive end. It paid off. He tied a team record with five sacks in a game against the Denver Broncos, and his 15 sacks were good for second in the NFL that season.

In 2016 Mack had 77 tackles (56 solo), 11 sacks, five forced fumbles and three fumble recoveries, and he ran an interception back for a touchdown. He also tied an NFL record with sacks in eight straight games, and the Raiders ended a streak of 14 years out of the playoffs.

Mack capped off the season as the 2016 Defensive Player of the Year, just the second Raider to win the award. He's also been named to three Pro Bowls and was a First Team All-Pro in 2015 and 2016. But he's still climbing that hill.

"I can get better," Mack said after being named Defensive Player of the Year. "I can get a whole lot better."

For quarterbacks looking across the line of scrimmage at the 6-foot-3, 250-pound bundle of fast-twitch muscle, that's a scary thought.

DEFENSE FIRST

In 2015 Mack became the first player in history to be named a First Team All-Pro at two positions (defensive end and linebacker) during the same season.

Khalil Mack is a one-man wrecking crew.

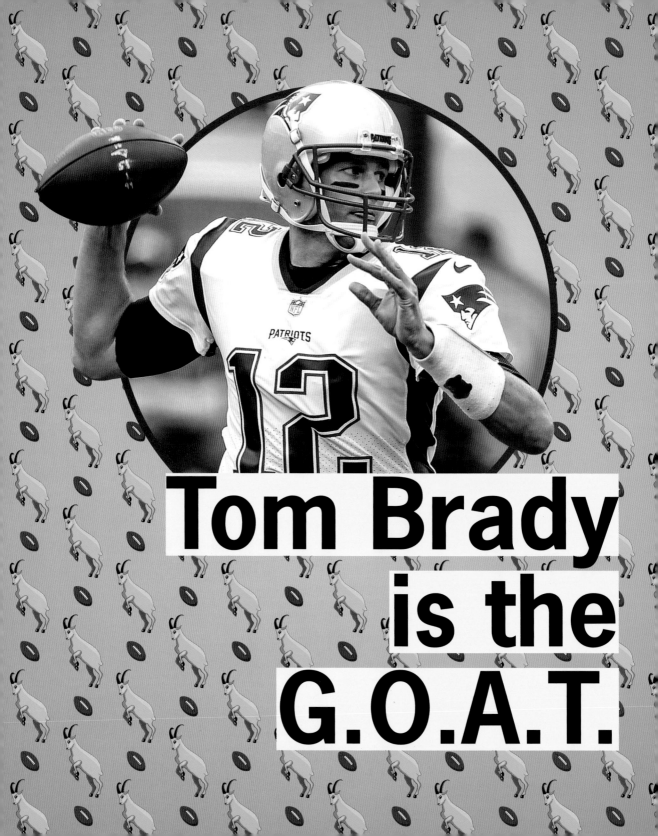

Tom Brady is the G.O.A.T.

Tom Brady
New England Patriots Quarterback

When Harry Kane scored his 100th goal, he wrote in *The Players' Tribune* that early in his career he had been inspired by Tom Brady.

Kane is an English striker who plays the international type of football (what we call soccer), so it's unusual that he'd look to the American kind of football for a hero. But Brady is the rare NFL player who has become a worldwide superstar.

"Brady believed in himself *so* much — and he just kept working and working, almost obsessively, in order to get better," said Kane.

He had to. Brady grew up in San Mateo, California, but went east to the University of Michigan. Considered skinny and slow, he was hardly the toast of Ann Arbor, but he was driven and learned to use people's doubts as motivation.

He was given even more fuel at the NFL draft: Brady had to wait until the sixth round in 2000 to be drafted by the New England Patriots. He was chosen 199th overall, with six quarterbacks taken ahead of him, but just one season later he was Super Bowl XXXVI champion and MVP.

After almost 20 years in the league, Brady's accomplishments and numbers are mind-boggling. In 2016 Brady passed Peyton Manning for most combined regular-season and playoff wins by a quarterback. In 2017 his 187th win broke the record for regular-season wins that had been held by Manning and Brett Favre. By the end of the 2017 season, Brady's regular-season wins had reached 196, including a 16-0 season and a record 31-game home winning streak.

But it's in the postseason that Brady really shines. In Super Bowl LI, the Patriots were down 28–3 in the third quarter, but Brady led them to 31 unanswered points to win 34–28. It was the first overtime win and biggest comeback in Super Bowl history. It was also Brady's fifth Super Bowl win, breaking a quarterback record held by Terry Bradshaw and his childhood hero, Joe Montana. He also passed Montana with his fourth Super Bowl MVP award to set a new mark.

A year later, the Patriots were in their eighth Super Bowl with Brady at the helm. They lost to the Philadelphia Eagles, but Brady threw for 505 yards, the most in Super Bowl history, and he became the first player to throw for over 10,000 yards in the postseason.

Just before the 2017 season, Brady turned 40 and was named the number one player on the NFL's Top 100 list. Defying father time and living up to his top billing, he led the NFL with 4,577 passing yards and won his third MVP award.

Brady is the oldest MVP winner in NFL history, and for one of the most famous athletes on the planet they could have added the title of G.O.A.T. — greatest of all time.

CAPTAIN CLUTCH

Brady ranks first in playoff history for starts by a quarterback (37), wins (27), passing yards (10,226), completions (920), touchdowns (71), multi-touchdown games (23) and 300-yard passing games (14).

Todd Gurley II
Los Angeles Rams
Running Back

30

When Todd Gurley was 6 years old, he was so good at football that they put him on a team with kids who were 9 to 11. He was the star of the team.

When he got to Tarboro High School in North Carolina though, he just wanted to play basketball. Halfway through the football season in his freshman year, the coach finally convinced him to play on the junior varsity team.

Promoted to varsity squad for the 2009 playoffs, Tarboro won the first of his three straight state championships. In the 2011 title game, Gurley rushed for 242 yards and four touchdowns, and he was later named North Carolina's Player of the Year.

At the University of Georgia, Gurley had a total of 3,285 rushing yards, 4,322 all-purpose yards and 44 touchdowns, all the second-highest totals in the school's history. His 6.44 yards per rush rank first.

The St. Louis Rams chose Gurley 10th overall in the 2015 draft, and he made an instant impact. His 566 yards rushing were the most in any player's first four games in the Super Bowl era (that is, since 1967), and he was the first rookie in history with four straight games of 125 or more yards rushing. He was also named the 2015 Offensive Rookie of the Year.

After the team moved to Los Angeles, Gurley won the 2017 Offensive Player of the Year award and was second in MVP voting. He led the NFL in rushing touchdowns (13), total touchdowns (19) and all-purpose yards (2,093).

Gurley was just the third player in history with at least 2,000 total yards, 10 rushing touchdowns and five receiving touchdowns in a season. And he did it without even playing the final game because the Rams had already clinched their first playoff berth since 2004.

"I really saw it early in him," said Jeff Craddock, his high school coach. "If he stays healthy, he's going to be a Hall of Fame running back in the NFL. I think he was my once-in-a-lifetime player."

Gurley is a pretty special person too. He wore cleats with the Shriners Hospitals for Children logo during the NFL's 2017 "My Cleats My Cause" week. He's the son of a single mom of four who worked nights as a nurse, and he chose to support the Shriners Hospitals after visiting the Chicago location when he was in college. "These kids fight day in and day out and it brings me joy knowing I can put a smile on their faces," he said.

When Gurley earned the most fantasy points in the NFL in 2017, grateful fantasy players sent some of their winnings to Shriners Hospitals. A spokesperson said they got so many donations in his name they thought he'd died.

Thankfully for the Rams and football fans everywhere, he is alive and doing very well.

ALL-AROUND ATHLETE | Gurley was a track star in high school and competed in hurdles at the 2011 World Youth Championships in France.

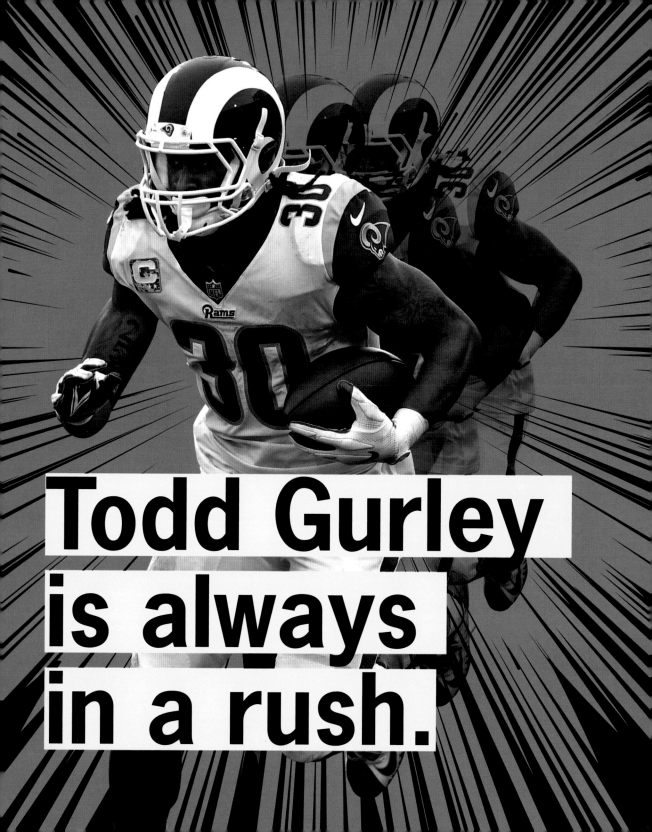

Todd Gurley
is always
in a rush.

Cameron Jordan
New Orleans Saints Defensive End

In 2014 Cameron Jordan made an appearance on the TV show *The League* with Jordan Cameron. One of the characters got them confused while drafting his fantasy league team, and then life imitated art in 2015. The Miami Dolphins announced they had signed defensive end Cameron Jordan as a free agent, but they had really signed tight end Jordan Cameron.

In the real NFL draft, Cameron Jordan was drafted by the New Orleans Saints 24th over-all in 2011 out of the University of California, Berkeley.

His father, Steve, played 13 seasons as a tight end with the Minnesota Vikings, but as a kid Cameron didn't really want to play football. He played the piano and tap danced, and when it came to sports he preferred basketball.

In eighth grade, he finally joined the football team. His dad told him he didn't have to play after that season if he didn't want to, and at first Jordan didn't try too hard. But by the end of the season, he was team captain.

At Chandler High School in Arizona, Jordan broke the career quarterback takedown record in one season. He was named an All-State as a senior and was also a state discus champion.

In the NFL, the 6-foot-4, 287-pound Jordan doesn't always get the credit he deserves. His position is measured by sacks, but that's just one part of his game. He does a bit of everything as the anchor of the Saints' defense, playing against the run or the pass with both speed and power.

In 2017 Jordan couldn't be ignored though. He played in 92 percent of the Saints' defensive plays, and he filled the stats sheet. Borrowing a basketball term, he earned what he called a "triple-double." He had 11 passes defensed (his career high) to go with his 18 tackles for a loss and 13.0 sacks, which tied for fourth in the league. That same year Jordan was chosen for his third Pro Bowl and was a First Team All-Pro for the very first time. He was also named the Saints' Walter Payton Man of the Year. He's never missed a game in his career, nor has he missed a chance to give back to his community.

Jordan has been the face of the Saints Kids Club for four years, and he often visits young patients at Ochsner Medical Center. He also gives motivational speeches to youth and high school students on topics close to his heart, like literacy, academics and fitness.

When discussing why he wants to help young people get a better start in life, Jordan explains, "At the end of the day, I'm doing it because it's the right thing to do. I'm not saying I'm the foundation — just a brick."

To the Saints and the city of New Orleans, he's more than that. He's a cornerstone.

SOME WINE WITH THAT BEEF?

Jordan and Carolina Panthers' quarterback Cam Newton have a friendly social media battle. After Jordan made fun of Newton's fashion choices, Newton said he'd send Jordan some "sauce," meaning style. After the Saints beat the Panthers in the 2017 playoffs, Jordan sent Newton his own sauce — in the form of a bottle of wine labeled "Jordan."

Matthew Stafford is Motor City money.

Matthew Stafford
Detroit Lions Quarterback

When sports fans go through decades of losing, they tend to blame curses. In baseball, the Boston Red Sox had the Curse of the Bambino and the Chicago Cubs had the Curse of the Billy Goat, but both of those have been broken. In the NFL, the Detroit Lions still have one — the Curse of Bobby Layne.

Layne was the last quarterback to win a title for the Lions, but the following year Layne was traded. On his way out of town he said the Lions wouldn't win for the next 50 years. In 2008, on the 50th anniversary of the curse, the Lions became the first team to finish a season 0-16. That got them the first overall draft pick in 2009, and they drafted Matthew Stafford, who had gone to Highland Park High School in Dallas, Texas — the same high school as Layne.

After three years and two Bowl victories at the University of Georgia, Stafford earned the Lions' starting job out of his first training camp. In the third game of the 2009 season, he helped them win their first game since 2007, and later that season the Stafford legend was born.

In a game against the Cleveland Browns, while wearing a microphone for NFL Films, Stafford set a rookie record with 422 yards passing. He badly injured his shoulder on the last play of the game, but the Browns were called for pass interference and he threw once more. It was a last-second touchdown, which tied the rookie record of five and clinched a 38–37 victory for the Lions. NFL Films president Steve Sabol said Stafford "earned a lasting place in the cinematic folklore of the NFL."

Stafford reinjured his shoulder in 2010 and played only three games, but in 2011 he set all-time single-season team records in completions (421), yards (5,038), touchdowns (41), completion percentage (63.5) and passer rating (97.2). Stafford was just the third quarterback in NFL history with 5,000-plus passing yards and 40-plus touchdowns in a season. The Lions made the playoffs for the first time since 1999.

In 2013 Stafford beat Layne's franchise mark for career passing yards. In 2014 he passed Layne with 131 career touchdowns, and he reached 20,000 passing yards in his 71st game, the fastest player in NFL history to get there. He was also quickest to reach 30,000 passing yards, hitting the mark in just 109 games.

In 2016 Stafford led the Lions to a record eight comeback wins in a fourth quarter or overtime, and the team earned another playoff berth. Detroit locked him down long-term, and he finished 2017 ranked third in the NFL in completions and yards and fourth in touchdowns.

Stafford has broken all of Layne's records, but the Lions still haven't won a championship since 1957. Now it's time to break the curse.

SOMETHING IN THE WATER

Growing up, Stafford played football and baseball with Los Angeles Dodgers pitcher Clayton Kershaw. When they signed their current contracts they were the highest-paid players in their respective sports.

J.J. Watt
Houston Texans
Defensive End

99

J.J. Watt barely got on the field in 2017, ▪ but *Sports Illustrated* still named him Sportsperson of the Year.

In August 2017, while he and his Houston Texans were out of town playing a preseason game, Hurricane Harvey left Houston devastated. The founder and namesake of the Justin J. Watt Foundation took it upon himself to be front and center during the recovery. Watt organized relief efforts and set a fundraising goal of $200,000. He inspired people of all ages across the country, and donations large and small rolled in. In the end, more than 200,000 people donated a total of over $37 million.

Two of the donors were Calvin and Corey Iverson. Their dad, Clay, had coached Watt back in Pewaukee, Wisconsin. In high school, Watt was a 5-foot-9 freshman quarterback who grew to be 6-foot-2 by his junior year. He was "all knees and elbows," according to Iverson, but he was determined and still growing.

In 2007 Watt played tight end at Central Michigan University. After deciding that didn't feel quite right, he went home to the University of Wisconsin to try out on defense for the Badgers. He made the cut and was named a Second Team All-American in 2010.

The Texans drafted Watt 11th overall in 2011, and in his first season he helped Houston go from 30th in the NFL in team defense to second. The following season Watt took the league by storm, leading the NFL with 20.5 sacks and winning Defensive Player of the Year. He did it again in 2014, this time with a clean sweep of the ballots, the first time in history that has happened. He was also second to Aaron Rodgers for MVP, earning 13 of the 50 votes, the most a defensive player had received since 1999.

Watt, called the "perfect football player" by former Texans coach Wade Phillips, added a third Defensive Player of the Year award in 2015. He is just the second player to win the honor three times.

After not missing a game in his first five seasons, Watt played only eight games in 2016 and 2017. In 2016 injuries took their toll, and Watt had surgery on his groin, abdomen and back. A couple weeks after Hurricane Harvey struck, the Texans opened the 2017 season at home, and Watt inspired Houston again when he came back for the first time in nearly a year. In the fifth game of the season, however, he suffered a serious knee injury and was done for the year.

Despite his broken body, Watt has helped repair his broken city, which is why *Sports Illustrated* called him "more than just the greatest defensive player of his generation."

Modestly, Watt says he simply gave people a way to donate: "If I'm going to get an award, I feel like over 200,000 other people should, too."

THAT'S OFFENSIVE!

In 2014, Watt had five touchdowns — three receiving, one on a fumble recovery and one from an interception. He was the first defensive lineman since 1944 to have five touchdowns in a season.

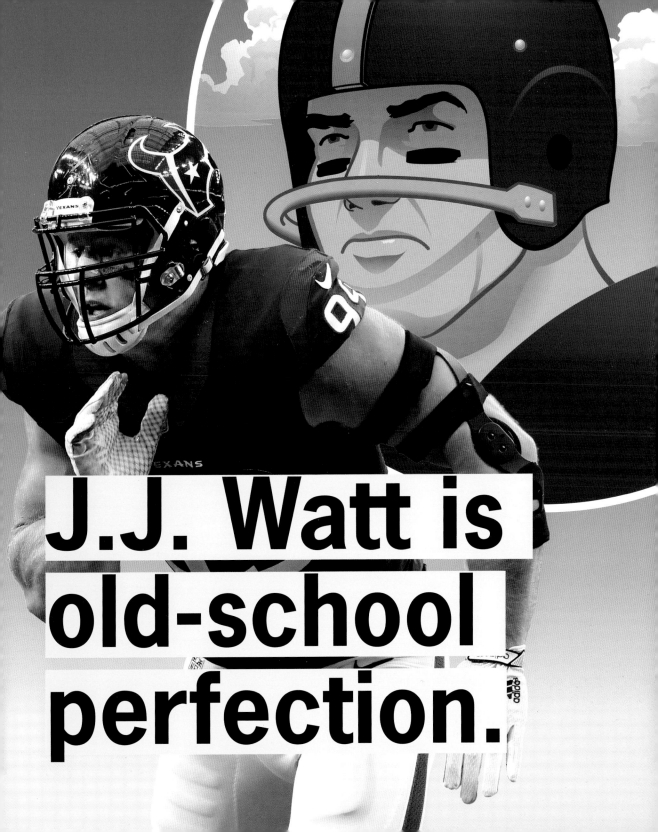

J.J. Watt is old-school perfection.

Cam Newton
Carolina Panthers Quarterback

C am Newton loves to play football, and he's always been pretty good at it. When he was graduating from Westlake High School in Atlanta, Georgia, he had more than 40 scholarship offers.

Most schools wanted Newton to be a tight end, but Blinn College in Brenham, Texas, knew he could do more. With some encouragement and faith in Newton's skill, they put him at quarterback, and he led them to the national junior college championship. After that, Division I Auburn University wanted him to lead their squad.

Newton had one of the best Division I seasons ever. He broke a bunch of school records, won the Heisman Trophy and brought Auburn its first national title since 1957.

The Carolina Panthers snapped him up with the number-one pick in the 2011 NFL draft, and in his first NFL game he threw for 422 yards. That broke Peyton Manning's record for most yards in a player's first game.

And he could run, too. That first season Newton set the record for rushing touchdowns by a quarterback, with 14. He was also the first quarterback in history with over 4,000 yards passing and 500 yards rushing in a season.

As a club, the Panthers came together around Newton. In 2013 they were 12-4 and won the NFC South title, and in 2014 they were the first team in the NFC South to repeat.

The Panthers were 15-1 in the 2015 regular season, and they had fun winning (even if they did lose in the Super Bowl). With Newton as their leader, the team celebrated touchdowns with group poses, while Newton did his best Superman impression. Newton had reason to celebrate: Carolina was the NFL's top-rated offense, and he had 35 touchdown passes and 10 rushing touchdowns.

With all that scoring there was also plenty of "Dabbin'" — the dance move was one of his favorite celebrations. Newton didn't invent the Dab, but Migos, the rap group who created it, have called him the "Dab Daddy." Some people thought Newton was disrespecting the game with the move, but he was just enjoying a historic season. MVP voters didn't hold it against him either — he got 48 out of 50 votes to win the 2015 award.

In 2016 Newton broke the NFL record for rushing touchdowns by a quarterback, with his 44th, but he'd retired the Dab. When he rushed for his 50th in 2017, he raised his fist instead to support other protesting players and celebrate in a socially conscious and positive way.

"The message is unity for me, black, white, different minorities around America," Newton said afterward. "That's my message. I want everybody to come together. We get nowhere separated."

OVER LAND AND THROUGH THE AIR

Newton has 37 career games with both a passing and a rushing touchdown — the most in NFL history!

Cam Newton is a touchdown machine.

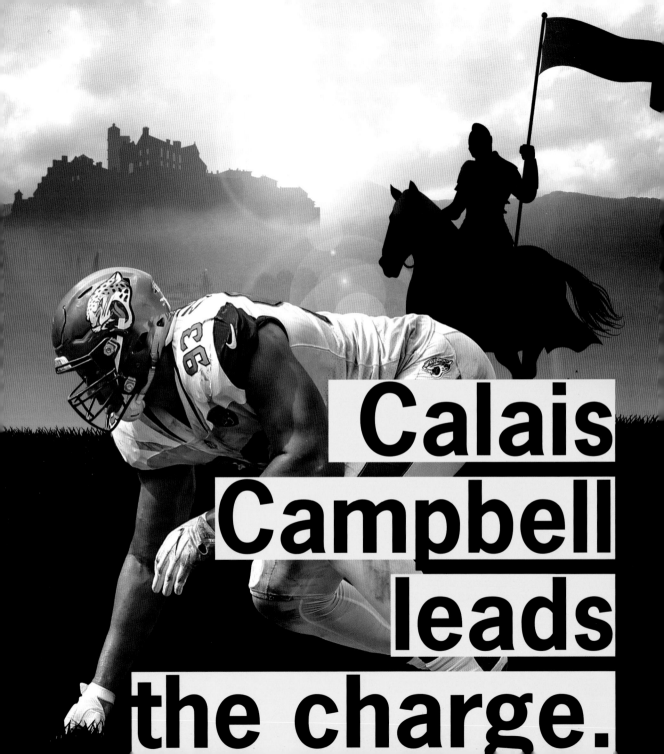

Calais Campbell leads the charge.

Calais Campbell
Jacksonville Jaguars
Defensive End

A lot of NFL players come from humble beginnings, but not many shared a room with nine other people. When he was 11 years old, Calais Campbell and his family lived in a homeless shelter in Denver. His parents and their eight children lived in one bedroom and shared one bathroom.

Embarrassed, Campbell hid his living situation from his friends until his family was able to move out. The tough situation bonded his family, and they're close to this day. He also credits it for his drive: "Looking back on it now, it really made me stronger," says Campbell. "It made me who I am today."

Who he is today is one of the NFL's biggest, strongest and most respected players.

His path to the NFL went through South High School in Aurora, Colorado. As a senior linebacker there he recorded 19 sacks, 188 tackles and two interceptions to earn a scholarship to the University of Miami.

While playing at Miami he totaled 158 tackles, 19.5 sacks and 39 tackles for a loss, but his impact went well beyond that. In 2015 he gave $1.6 million to the school, the largest donation a former student-athlete had ever given.

In 2008 the Arizona Cardinals drafted Campbell in the second round, 50th overall. He spent nine years in Arizona and set a team record by averaging at least 50 tackles and six sacks per season from 2009 to 2014.

Campbell reached second on the team's career sacks list with 56.5. He also had 492 tackles, 32 batted passes, eight forced fumbles, eight fumble recoveries, six blocked field goals and three interceptions. His last interception was during his Cardinals finale in 2016, and he returned it for his first career touchdown.

The Jacksonville Jaguars signed Campbell as a free agent in 2017, so he could be a veteran leader on an up-and-coming team.

And what a way to start: In the season opener, Campbell set a single-game team record with four sacks. By the end of the year he had 14.5 sacks, a new Jaguars single-season record. It was 5.5 more than his previous high and tied him for second in the NFL.

The Pro Football Writers of America named Campbell the Defensive Player of the Year, and he was a First Team All-Pro. More importantly for Campbell, who's always been a team player, he helped the Jaguars earn respect and the nickname "Sacksonville." He also led them all the way to the AFC championship game, their first since 1999.

Campbell received the 2015 Pop Warner Humanitarian Award, given to a player for both athletic achievement and community service. It's also for inspiring youth, something Campbell does by never forgetting his own childhood.

LIKE WALTER PAYTON, BUT BIGGER

A giant at 6-foot-8 and 300 pounds, Campbell has a heart to match. He was twice named the Cardinals' Walter Payton Man of the Year for his work with the Charles Richard Campbell Foundation, which he named after his father.

Aaron Rodgers is cool under pressure.

Aaron Rodgers
Green Bay Packers Quarterback

Aaron Rodgers was a skinny kid with huge feet (size 14!) and a strong arm. As the senior quarterback at Pleasant Valley High School in Chico, California, he set a school record for passing yards, but only one college coach was interested in him. And all that coach had to do to recruit him was cross the street!

Rodgers' neighbor Craig Rigsbee coached at tiny Butte College a few miles away, in Oroville, California. During his first season there, Rodgers led the Roadrunners to a 10-1 record. University of California, Berkeley, a Division I school, liked what they saw and invited Rodgers to play on the big stage. He went on to become the highest-rated passer in UC Berkeley's history.

It's a good thing Rodgers has big feet: he had big cleats to fill in Green Bay after the Packers picked him 24th overall in the 2005 draft. At the time, Green Bay quarterback Brett Favre had played every game for 16 seasons, won three NFL MVP awards and set NFL career records for completions, yards and touchdowns.

But Rodgers was used to proving himself, and in 2008 the Packers handed him the job after a messy split with Favre. Two years later, Rodgers led Green Bay to victory in Super Bowl XLV. He was also named the game's MVP.

In 2011, the same year that Tom Brady and Drew Brees both broke Dan Marino's 27-year-old passing record, Rodgers won the regular-season MVP award. He did it by setting the single-season quarterback rating record of 122.5, with 45 touchdowns and only six interceptions, as the Packers finished 15-1.

Wisconsin's state assembly celebrated by naming December 12, 2012 — 12/12/12 — Aaron Rodgers Day.

However, success leads to sky-high expectations. A slow start in 2014 had Packers fans pushing the panic button. Rodgers went on the radio and told fans to "R-E-L-A-X. Relax. We're going to be okay." Sure enough, the Packers won 11 of their next 13 games and the NFC North title, and Rodgers was named MVP again.

In 2016 Rodgers led the NFL with 40 touchdown passes, and he now has the highest career passer rating in NFL history (103.8) and the lowest interception percentage ever (1.6%). In addition to all of those honors, Rodgers received the 2014 Bart Starr Award, which is given to the player who exhibits character and leadership both on the field and in the community.

The 2017 season, however, got off to a rough start. In the sixth game of the season, Rodgers broke his right collarbone. He was supposed to miss the rest of the year, but he miraculously came back two months later — with screws holding his bone together. This difficult time only added to the legend of the scrawny kid from the little school who became one of America's biggest stars.

BRAWN & BRAINS!

In 2015, Rodgers beat Kevin O'Leary from *Shark Tank* and astronaut Mark Kelly on *Celebrity Jeopardy!* to win $50,000 for the Midwest Athletes Against Childhood Cancer (MACC) Fund.

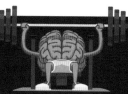

Odell Beckham Jr.
New York Giants
Wide Receiver

13

On November 23, 2014, New York Giants receiver Odell Beckham Jr. left his feet and dove backward with a defender all over him. He reached behind his head with his back parallel to the ground and snagged an Eli Manning pass with little more than his index finger. He landed in the end zone, and social media blew up.

The memes went viral, including Beckham superimposed into the film *Dirty Dancing* and onto the ceiling of the Sistine Chapel. There were 23,000 tweets per minute about the catch, and he had 686,000 Twitter mentions and 62,726 new followers within 24 hours.

In traditional media, NBC analyst Cris Collinsworth, who played eight years at wide receiver, said, "That may be the greatest catch I've ever seen. You have to be kidding me!"

But Beckham was born to perform such feats. His dad, Odell Sr., was a running back at Louisiana State University, and his mom, Heather Van Norman, won three NCAA titles as a member of the LSU relay team.

There was little doubt Odell Jr. would be an LSU Tiger after graduating from Isidore Newman High School in New Orleans.

In three seasons at LSU, Beckham had 143 receptions for 2,340 yards and 12 touchdowns. He also returned 42 kickoffs for 1,044 yards (an average of 24.9 yards per kickoff) and 62 punts for 557 yards and two touchdowns. Those impressive totals earned him the Paul Hornung Award as the NCAA's most versatile football player.

The Giants chose Beckham 12th overall in 2014 NFL draft. He was on the inactive list for the first four games with a hamstring tear, but the rest of his season was momentous.

His acrobatic index-finger catch was part of a 10-reception, 146-yard day, and he finished the season with 1,305 yards and a league-leading 108.8 yards per game. He was the first receiver in history to reach 1,000 yards after missing the season's first three games, and he became the first Giant to be named the NFL's Offensive Rookie of the Year.

Until a gruesome ankle injury in his fourth game of the 2017 season, Beckham had kept up his historic receiving rate. He's the only player in history with at least 85 receptions, 1,000 yards and 10 touchdowns in each of his first three seasons, and he played in the Pro Bowl each of those seasons. He was also quickest in NFL history to both 200 receptions and 3,000 yards.

Beckham, who spent a summer house-sitting Drake's "YOLO Estate," aspires to the musician's level of professional success. And with his signature blonde Mohawk, he's almost as recognizable as Drake on the street. With a few more receptions like the one that launched his career, he'll catch up to him in Twitter followers too.

A WISH COME TRUE

Beckham hosts a child from the Make-A-Wish Foundation at every home game. He brings them to the team's Saturday walk-through and plays catch with them on the field after the game.

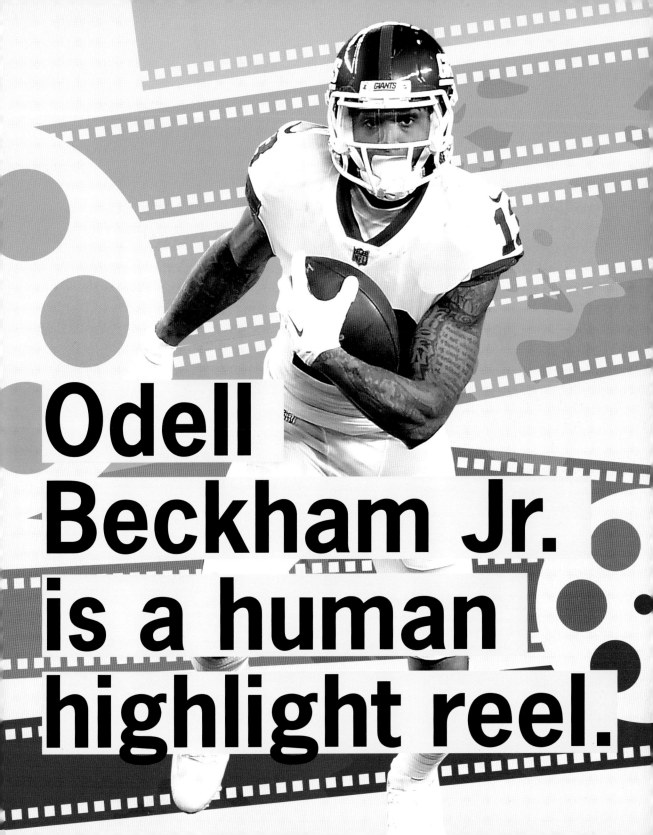

Odell Beckham Jr. is a human highlight reel.

Russell Wilson's persistence pays off.

Russell Wilson
Seattle Seahawks
Quarterback

Russell Wilson's dad, Harrison, used to wake him up at 5:30 every morning to work out and run drills, always stressing the importance of poise and preparation. It paid off in his senior year at private Collegiate High School in Richmond, Virginia. Wilson led his football team to the state title, and he batted .467 as the starting shortstop on the baseball team.

Major League Baseball's Colorado Rockies thought he had a future and drafted him in 2010. Wilson had dreams of being like Bo Jackson and Deion Sanders, who both played pro baseball and football. His college football coach at North Carolina State didn't like that idea, so Wilson transferred to the University of Wisconsin. He worked his schedule to play minorleague baseball when the football team wasn't playing, but ultimately he chose the gridiron.

A pro football career wasn't a given, however. Even though he set an NCAA record by throwing 379 passes in a row without an interception, Wilson's 5-foot-11 frame scared many NFL teams, who thought he was too short. The Seahawks liked what they saw though, and they drafted him in the third round in 2012.

Wilson started all 16 games of his first year and tied Peyton Manning's rookie record of 26 touchdown passes. He set a franchise record with a 100.0 quarterback rating — the second highest by a first-year player in NFL history.

In 2013 the Seahawks won 11 of their first 12 games and beat Manning and the Denver Broncos 43–8 to win Super Bowl XLVIII. Wilson completed 72% of his passes, with two touchdowns and a 123.1 passer rating.

Wilson was enjoying his success, hanging out with Barack Obama, Justin Bieber and Beyoncé. He'd gone from too small to a megastar in 24 months. The Texas Rangers also picked up his baseball rights, and he's twice participated in their spring training.

In 2014 the Seahawks made their way back to the Super Bowl, and with only a few yards between him and back-to-back titles, Wilson had his go-ahead touchdown pass intercepted and the New England Patriots won Super Bowl XLIX. While others blamed the coaching, Wilson took "full responsibility" for the play and said it was part of God's plan.

Wilson played through injuries in 2016, but he hasn't missed a game in his career. He's fanatical with his training, which has made the undersized quarterback one of the giants of the game.

"I want to be the best in the world," says Wilson, who was first in the NFL in both passing touchdowns (34) and passer rating (110.1) in 2017, earning him his fourth Pro Bowl nod, while he also led the Seahawks in rushing yards. "That's the truth. I try to strive for that. Every day. Every morning I wake up. Every night. Every offseason. Every year."

RACING UP THE RECORD BOOK

Wilson set a record for the fastest quarterback to 50 wins, and his 65 wins are the most by any quarterback in their first six seasons. He's also the quickest quarterback to 150 passing touchdowns and 3,000 rushing yards, achieving those marks in 91 career games.

Luke Kuechly
Carolina Panthers
Linebacker

59

Luke Kuechly — pronounced KEEK-lee — is a tackle machine and a record smasher, and no one saw it coming. Not even his parents.

Growing up in Evendale, Ohio, Kuechly played for the St. Xavier High School team. In his junior year they went undefeated and won the state championship, and afterward his coach told his parents to expect a lot of calls from colleges. Eileen Kuechly says she remembers thinking, "You don't know what you're talking about. That's crazy."

It wasn't. Kuechly had a dominant senior season, and the University of Cincinnati offered him a scholarship. He didn't want to stay so close to home though, and he was looking for the best possible education. After considering Duke and Stanford, he chose Boston College.

As a junior, Kuechly won the Bronko Nagurski Trophy as the nation's top defensive player and the Butkus Award as the most outstanding linebacker. He was also named a First Team All-American for the third time.

Kuechly left college after his junior year, and the Carolina Panthers drafted him ninth overall in 2012. After he moved to his natural middle linebacker position in the fifth game of his rookie year, the Panthers jumped all the way from 24th in the league defensively to 10th.

He played every snap the rest of the season at middle linebacker and led the league in tackles with 164, breaking the NFL rookie record and earning him the 2012 Defensive Rookie of the Year award. Even his mom finally admitted that her son belonged, saying to his high school coach, "I have to apologize to you because I thought you were nuts."

Kuechly is now a bonafide NFL star. He was named the 2013 Defensive Player of the Year, helped the Panthers reach Super Bowl 50 in 2016 (which they lost to the Denver Broncos), has been an All-Pro four times and played in five Pro Bowls.

Kuechly is also a spokesperson for Project Life, an organization that helps register college students for bone marrow and tissue donations. "The first person I thought of was Luke Kuechly," says CEO Steve Luquire. "He's an impressive young man. I know enough people at the Panthers who say what a quality individual he is."

Panthers quarterback Cam Newton calls him "Captain America" because of his good looks, positive attitude and superhuman abilities on the field.

"He's so friendly," says Newton, "like extremely friendly. ... You would never think in a million years a guy like Luke Kuechly, the way he looks in everyday life, is one of if not the best defensive player in the National Football League."

AWARDS SEASON

Kuechly is the second player in NFL history to win Defensive Rookie of the Year and Defensive Player of the Year in back-to-back seasons, and he's just the eighth to win both during his career.

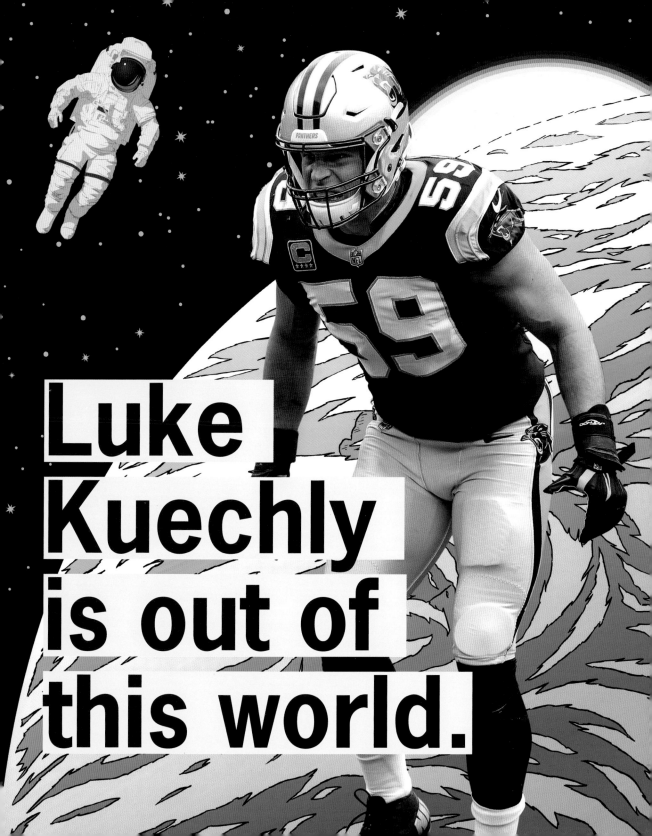

Luke
Kuechly
is out of
this world.

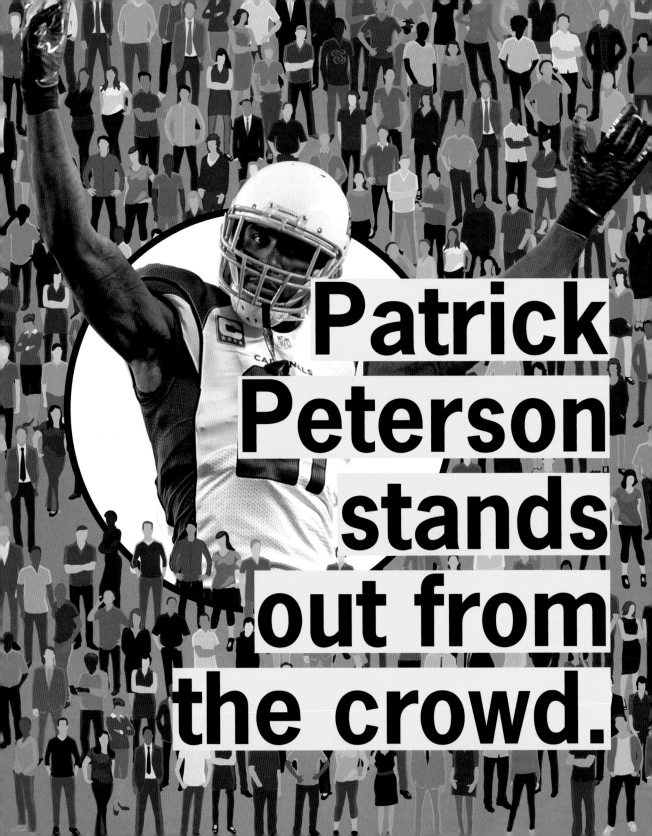

Patrick Peterson stands out from the crowd.

The NFL's Walter Payton Man of the Year Award recognizes excellence both on the field and in the community. Patrick De'mon Peterson couldn't be a better example of that combination.

In 2017 Peterson was named the Arizona Cardinals' Man of the Year for the second time. It was a salute to his Foundation for Success, which he started in 2013 to give low-income youth opportunities and resources. He has since added two other programs: Patrick's Corner, which gives young people a safe space to read in schools and community centers, and the Pick Out a Book program. Peterson didn't stop there, however. In 2017 he provided Thanksgiving meals for over 200 families in Arizona and visited Haiti with Mission of Hope.

In 2016 Peterson provided clothing and school supplies for kids in Baton Rouge, Louisiana, after it was devastated by floods. The city is close to his heart because it's where he became a college star.

At Blanche Ely High School in Pompano Beach, Florida, Peterson was named *USA Today* Defensive Player of the Year and an All-American. He chose Louisiana State University, and in his final season he won both the Chuck Bednarik Award as the country's best defender and the Jim Thorpe Award as top defensive back.

Peterson was drafted fifth overall by the Arizona Cardinals in 2011. In his first season he had 699 punt return yards (a rookie record) and scored four punt return touchdowns, both of which led the NFL that season. After only 11 games, Peterson had set the Cardinals' career

Patrick Peterson
Arizona Cardinals
Cornerback

21

mark for punt return touchdowns. He also tied the single-season NFL record, and he was the first in history with four return touchdowns in a season of 80 or more yards. That debut helped make him a 2011 All-Rookie and First Team All-Pro.

In 2013 and 2015 Peterson was named a First Team All-Pro again, this time at the cornerback position. In 2017 he was named to his seventh straight Pro Bowl, one for each season he'd been in the NFL. He's only the second player in history to be an All-Star on defense and as a kick returner.

Peterson has never missed a game, and he's been voted one of the top 100 players for six straight years. For the last three years he's been in the top 20.

Asked about Peterson, New York Giants star receiver Odell Beckham Jr. said, "By far just one of the best in the game, hands down."

Peterson's play has earned him many more compliments and honors, but that's not what's most important to him: "It means more to me to be a better person than a better football player," he says, "because that lasts longer."

BLOOD SUGAR BATTLES

In 2015 Peterson found out he has type-2 diabetes, which had made him gain weight and slowed him down over the course of the 2014 season. After changing his diet he went back to his high school weight, regained his energy and declared "The Ferrari is back!"

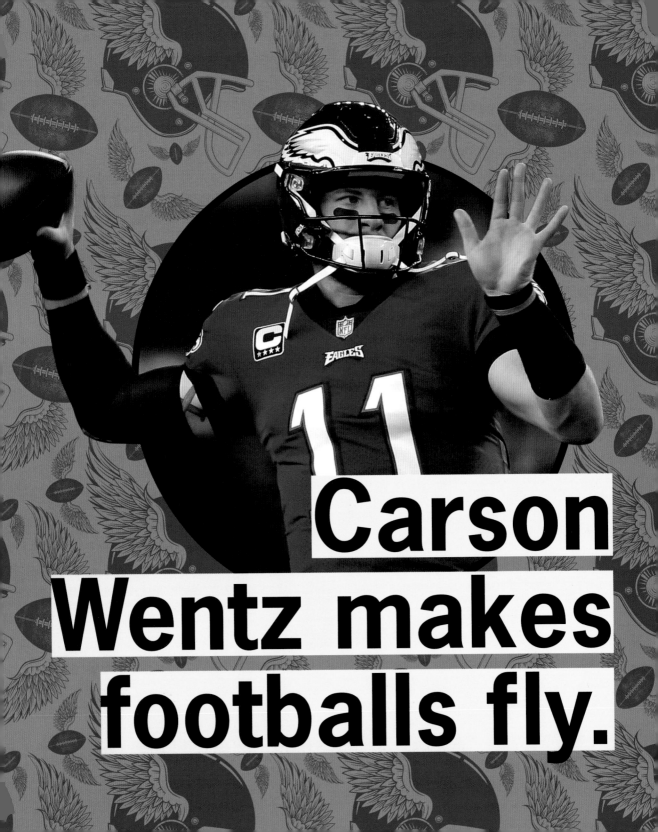

Carson Wentz makes footballs fly.

Carson Wentz
Philadelphia Eagles Quarterback

Late in the third quarter of a game in 2017, the Philadelphia Eagles' Carson Wentz was hit from both sides as he dove into the end zone. He crossed the goal line, but the touchdown was called back on a holding penalty. Three plays later he stood in the pocket and threw a touchdown pass to Alshon Jeffery to give the Eagles the lead. It turned out that he was standing on a torn ACL, which cost him the rest of the season.

With that 43–35 win over the Los Angeles Rams, the Eagles clinched the NFC East division championship with three games to spare. Heroic performances like this one made Wentz a leading candidate for MVP in just his second year in the NFL. When his season ended early, he had 33 touchdown passes, which was tops in the NFL. Even with the lost games, he finished the year second in the league. He also set an Eagles' record, beating Sonny Jurgensen's 32 touchdowns from 1961.

Wentz was just the third quarterback in NFL history with at least 33 touchdown passes and seven interceptions or less. The other two are future Hall of Famers Tom Brady and Aaron Rodgers, so it's safe to say the Eagles are satisfied with the moves they made to get Wentz.

In 2016 Philadelphia traded five draft picks in order to move up and choose Wentz second overall. He was the highest drafted quarterback from a Football Championship Subdivision school (the second tier in American college football) in history.

Wentz, who grew up in Bismarck, North Dakota, had a record of 20-3 as starting quarterback at North Dakota State, where he led the team to two FCS national championships.

The Eagles had their quarterback of the future. Wentz started all 16 games in 2016, threw for nearly 4,000 yards and set an NFL rookie record with 379 completions.

In the offseason Wentz went to Haiti with a Christian organization called Mission of Hope. It inspired him to start the Carson Wentz AO1 Foundation, which stands for Wentz's Audience of One — Jesus. His organization helps support underprivileged youth, provides outdoor opportunities to veterans and people who face challenges, and supplies service dogs to people in need.

Although an injury ended his breakthrough 2017 season, the Eagles' savior proved he belongs among the NFL elite. But this man of faith knows there's more to life than football: "On the field, and in everything I do, honestly, [my faith] gives me a bigger picture," says Wentz. "So when I'm playing football and it's good, bad or ugly, I realize I'm not trying to please the fans or the media."

Just his Audience of One.

GROWTH SPURT! | As a freshman in high school, Wentz was 5-foot-8. By the time he graduated as valedictorian of his class, he was 6-foot-5.

Tyron Smith
Dallas Cowboys
Offensive Tackle

77

Legendary basketball coach John Wooden said, "The true test of a man's character is what he does when no one is watching."

It means that when the only person making sure you do the right thing is you, do you still work hard and make the right choices?

In Tyron Smith's case, he's a huge man who does his best work out of the spotlight. He plays for the Dallas Cowboys, America's most popular team. However, as a tackle on the offensive line, Smith's hard work can go largely unnoticed. It's other people who get the benefit — and with Smith, it's been this way since he was a little kid.

From an early age, he and his siblings worked in his family's cleaning business. They'd drive hours from their home to prepare new houses for the owners. After working through the night, the family would get home just before the sun came up, and then young Tyron would go to school.

In elementary school, Smith was too busy cleaning to play football, but by the time he got to Rancho Verde High in Moreno Valley, it was hard to ignore his size and skill. It earned him a scholarship to the University of Southern California, where he was an All-American and the conference's top offensive lineman.

Smith was drafted ninth overall in 2011 by the Dallas Cowboys. At 20 years old, he was the youngest player in the NFL that year. He started all 16 games of his first season at right tackle and allowed only three sacks.

True to form, Smith has continued to do the dirty work while making others look good. In 2014 he blocked for DeMarco Murray, the NFL's rushing leader and the second-ranked running back in the league. He protected quarterback Tony Romo, helping him become the most efficient passer in both the Cowboys' and the league's history (69.9 completion percentage and 113.2 rating). Smith's blocking also enabled wide receiver Dez Bryant to score 16 touchdowns, which led all NFL receivers in 2014.

Two years later, Smith proved it wasn't a fluke. Dallas was second in the league in rushing again, but this time teammate Ezekiel Elliott was the NFL rushing king. Smith also guarded first-year quarterback Dak Prescott, who set league rookie records in quarterback rating (104.9) and completion percentage (67.8) and was just the second player and first rookie with 3,500-plus passing yards and fewer than five interceptions.

Smith isn't toiling in complete anonymity though. He's been a First Team All-Pro selection twice and has been named to the Pro Bowl each of the last five seasons. The Cowboys also appreciate his efforts, having signed him through 2023. They know the man who can bench press 600 pounds is doing their heavy lifting.

THE DOG DAYS OF DALLAS

Smith and his girlfriend have five rescue dogs, and in 2015 they created a fundraising calendar with Cowboys players hanging out with dogs to benefit a local shelter.

HiGH FiVE

Tyron Smith is a QB's best friend.

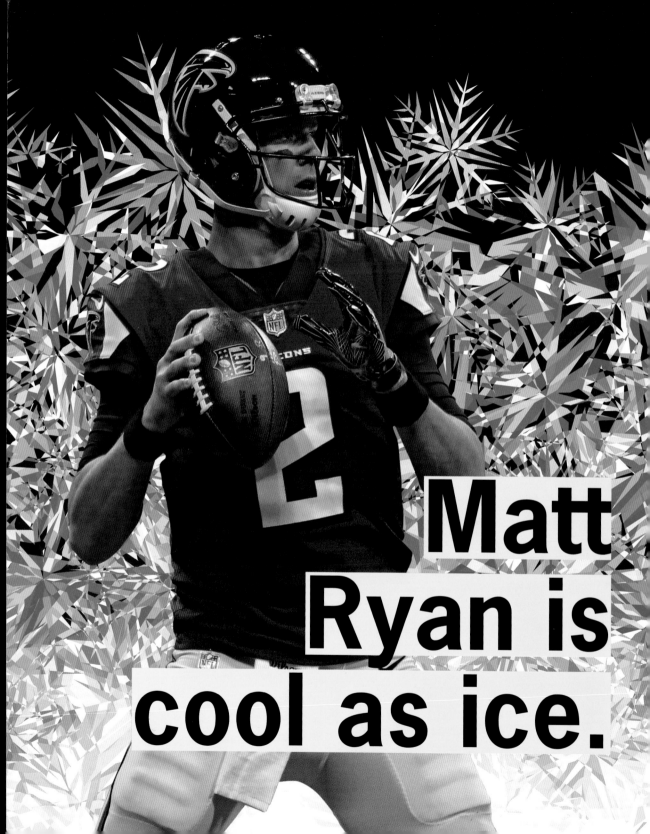

Matt Ryan is cool as ice.

Matt Ryan
Atlanta Falcons
Quarterback

I n college Matt Ryan was teased about how skinny he was. But when his teammates gave him their best shot in practice and he gave it back harder, he changed their minds.

"Holy smokes, this kid is going to be a player," left guard Ryan Poles remembers thinking.

And Matt Ryan is a player. He was captain of the baseball, basketball and football teams at William Penn Charter School in Philadelphia before he followed in the footsteps of his uncle John Loughery, a Boston College quarterback from 1979 to 1982.

At college Ryan broke many of Doug Flutie's school records, including single-season passing yards (4,507), career completions (807) and games with 400-plus yards passing (five).

Ryan also earned his "Matty Ice" nickname for his poise under pressure and toughness. After breaking his foot in 2006, he told the team trainer he was going to keep playing, which he did for the rest of the season. "It's already broken, so I'm not going to break it worse, right?" was his explanation.

In 2007 Ryan won the Manning Award as the nation's top quarterback and the Johnny Unitas Golden Arm Award, which is based on performance, character, leadership and academics.

It was a convincing case for the Atlanta Falcons, who picked Ryan third overall in the 2008 draft. His first NFL pass was a 65-yard touchdown, and at the end of the season he was named the NFL's Offensive Rookie of the Year.

After going 4-12 in 2007, the Falcons had an 11-5 record in 2008 with Ryan at the helm. They made the playoffs for the first time since 2004, and Ryan became the first rookie quarterback in history to start all 16 games and lead his team to the playoffs (which Joe Flacco also did that year).

In 2013 Ryan became the franchise leader in career completions and yards, and in 2016 he topped all of his own single-season records. He had 4,944 passing yards, 38 touchdowns and a 69.9 completion percentage. His 117.1 passer rating ranked first that season and fifth all-time.

Ryan was named NFL MVP, and a day after receiving the award the Falcons played the New England Patriots in Super Bowl LI. His rating for the game was 144.1, the fourth best in Super Bowl history, but the Falcons lost in overtime.

"Don't feel sorry for us," Ryan wrote in *The Players' Tribune*, "because we don't feel sorry for ourselves. … Losing the Super Bowl is always going to be a part of our story. But it's not our whole story."

Ryan is strong and ready to move the Falcons forward, as he's done so well for ten seasons, "Because the only fight that matters is the one you're in."

THE WING OF A FALCON

Ryan threw for over 4,000 yards for the seventh straight season in 2017, and he has over 41,000 passing yards in his career. That's more than 23 miles!

Antonio Brown
Pittsburgh Steelers
Wide Receiver

84

Antonio Brown grew up in a rough part of Miami, sometimes without a place to sleep. His dad — "Touchdown" Eddie Brown — was named the best player in Arena Football League history, but he wasn't around to help raise his son.

Brown's dream was to play in the NFL, but without a mom and dad to support him, his school grades suffered: "I wasn't a kid who got in trouble [or] did anything wrong," Brown says, "I just was a guy who didn't really have the right guidance in place and the right support [to help me do] the things that I wanted to do."

In high school Brown was one of the best sprinters in Florida and an All-State quarterback, even though he was so skinny he was called "Boney Tony." His small size and poor grades meant he didn't receive any scholarship offers, but he worked on his grades and eventually landed a tryout with Central Michigan University as a wide receiver. He made it and went on to become the only player in the school's history to have two 1,000-yard receiving seasons and two 100-reception seasons.

Brown was still scrawny though, so he wasn't picked until the sixth round of the 2010 NFL draft. The Pittsburgh Steelers took him 195th overall, and he sat on the bench for seven games in his rookie year.

"Patience," says Brown, "builds perseverance and it builds humility and it teaches you a lot."

His patience was rewarded in the playoffs. Brown made two unbelievable catches that helped the Steelers reach Super Bowl XLV. They lost to the Green Bay Packers, but the next year Brown became the first player in NFL history with at least 1,000 receiving yards and 1,000 return yards in the same season.

In 2013 Brown set a team record with 1,499 receiving yards and had the second-most receptions (110) in the team's history. In 2014 he blew those numbers away, leading the NFL with 129 receptions for 1,698 yards. In 2015 he was back in the record books with 136 catches (tied for second in NFL history) and 1,834 yards (fourth in NFL history). He was the first player to ever have at least 125 receptions in two straight seasons.

Since then, Brown has just kept adding to his highlight reel. Late in the 2017 season he had his 700th reception in his 111th career game, making him the quickest to reach that milestone. He finished the year tops in the NFL in receiving yards again, with 1,533. He's been in six Pro Bowls and a First Team All-Pro for four years and counting.

Even at the top of the game, Brown still uses the same mantra he did when he was a kid: "Chest up, eyes up, prayed up." With it, he says, "I have what it takes to move forward and get the good out of any situation that may hinder me ... it provides me with peace."

RECORD RECEPTIONS

On December 4, 2017, Brown made his 596th catch since 2013, totaling 7,611 receiving yards. In doing so, he set NFL records for the most catches and the highest number of receiving yard in a five-season stretch.

Photo Credits

Associated Press

Al Messerschmidt: 15 (Super Bowl XVII); AP Photo: 13 (Berwanger), 15 (Super Bowl I); Jeffrey Boan: 16 (Shula); NFL Photos: 14 (Gehrke); Pro Football Hall of Fame: 12 (Heffelfinger, Lambeau, Pollard), 13 (Nevers); Tom DiPace: 37 (Jordan)

Icon Sportswire

Andrew Dieb: 56 (Wentz), 59 (Smith); Andy Lewis: 3, 49 (Odell Jr.); Bob Falcetti: 15 (Grier); Cliff Welch: 41 (Watt); Chris Williams: 4, 35 (Gurley); Daniel Gluskoter: 20 (Fitzgerald), 31 (Mack), 46 (Rodgers); David Rosenblum: 44 (Campbell); Drew Hallowell: 16 (Smith); Hector Acevedo/Zuma Press: 50 (Wilson); James Allison: 26 (Sherman); Jim Dedmon: 53 (Kuechly); Jordon Kelly: 10; Joshua Sarner: 32 (Brady); Mark LoMoglio: 28 (Jones); MSA: 25 (Brees); Patrick Gorski: 11 (Huddle), 38 (Stafford); Rich Gabrielson: 23 (Miller); Rich Graessle: 8 (Vince Lombardi Trophy), 17 (Brady), 43 (Newton); Rich Kane: 16 (Manning); Robin Alam: 63 (Brown); Todd Kirkland: 60 (Ryan)

Shutterstock

Agor2012: 43 (background); Alexander_P: 28 (background); alexandrovskyi: 57 (height measure); Anikei: 25 (target); Antonov Maxim: 11 (griddle); armo.rs: 17 (flaming football); Artisticco: 13 (ball and goal post), 14 (helmet); aurielaki: 5 (field); bazzier: 13 (bear); Bogdan Syrotynskyi: 53 (astronaut); Christiaan Lloyd: 12 (rugby ball); Danomyte: 53 (background); Denis Maliugin: 14 (whistle); denk creative: 33 (hat); Dolimac: 23 (background); Doloves: 38 (money); doodle: 7 (referee); eatcute: 5 (stopwatch); FMStox: 11 (ball and goal post), 24 (football); gigirosado: 14 (television), 15 (television); Gocili: 6 (player outlines); gst: 61 (winged football); HelgaMariah: 55 (glucose meter); Hierarch: 48 (stars); Iconic Bestiary: 47 (brain); Illustratiostock: 6–7 (field), 7 (goal post); Jelica Videnovic: 15 (TV ratings); Jemastock: 17 (measuring tape); johavel: 13 (trophy), 45 (trophy); jorgen mcleman: 31 (background); Julia Waller: 56 (background); KannaA: 35 (background); kateetc: 36 (wine); kavalenkava: 58 (dog); klerik78: 7 (yard markers), 29 (yard markers); Ksanawo: 8 (small player); Luchenko Yana: 14 (foam hand); lukeruk: 49 (background); Macrovector: 30 (fence), 62 (hands); Maike Hildebrandt: 12 (rule book); Makkuro GL: 38 (cars); Marina Sun: 26 (background); Martial Red: 16 (website pointer); m.ekzarkho: 22 (suit); Melenay: 8 (large player); Michael Jaszewski: 41 (background); MSSA: 50 (background); NotionPic: 21 (superhero); OnBlast: 27 (school supplies); patrimonio designs ltd: 12 (player illustration); polygraphus: 60 (background); premiumicon: 16 (football outline); PremiumVector: 16 (clapping hands); Primsky: 37 (background); Rene Martin: 42 (foam hand), 51 (foam hand); RomanYa: 63 (background); rudall30: 44 (background); Rybakova: 32 (background); SaveJungle: 46 (background); Sentavio: 5 (players); Steinar: 6 (touchdown player), 40 (touchdown player); studiostoks: 59 (background); takiwa: 20 (background); Teerapol24: 52 (award); TesL: 62 (ball); T-Kot: 8 (trophy); Tomacco: 13 (radio); 14 (two helmets); TopVectorElements: 39 (faucet); Vaskina mat: 7 (ball), 9 (balls); Vector Tradition: 14 (football with laurels); whitehoune: 54 (background); Zmiter: 34 (shoes)

Cover

Icon Sportswire: Icon Sportswire (Brady), Rich Graessle (Kuechly), Robin Alam (Brown) Shutterstock: RomanYa (background)

Back Cover

Icon Sportswire: Chris Williams (Gurley), Daniel Gluskoter (Rodgers), Rich Gabrielson (Miller) Shutterstock: KannaA (Gurley background)